COLORADO REFLECTIONS

Photography by John Fielder
With Selected Prose & Poetry

❧ ❧

Colorado Littlebooks

WESTCLIFFE PUBLISHERS

Englewood, Colorado

First frontispiece: Engineer Mountain, San Juan Mountains
Second frontispiece: Ice Lakes Basin, above Silverton
Third frontispiece: The Ruby Mountains, above Crested Butte
Opposite: Along the East Fork of Avalanche Creek, Maroon Bells-Snowmass Wilderness

International Standard Book Number: 1-56579-054-5
Library of Congress Catalog Number: 94-060027
Copyright John Fielder, 1994. All rights reserved.
Published by Westcliffe Publishers, Inc.
2650 South Zuni Street, Englewood, Colorado 80110
Publisher, John Fielder; Editor, Suzanne Venino; Designer, Leslie Gerarden
Printed in Hong Kong by Palace Press

For more information about other fine books and calendars from Westcliffe Publishers,
please contact your local bookstore or contact us by calling (303) 935-0900,
faxing (303) 935-0903, or writing us for a free color catalogue.

PREFACE

❧❧

For 20 years I have been photographing Colorado's scenery, its flowers and mountains, rivers and canyons, lakes and creeks. If there is any one kind of photograph that has become common to all of these natural features, it would have to be my reflection images. The sight of a gorgeous peak at sunrise reflected in still waters is just too much beauty to resist. I guess I just like to get two for the price of one!

Calm waters untouched by the direct light of the sun make mirror images. Perfect conditions will create reflections that are no less sharp or vivid than their reflected land forms. Mornings and evenings are the best time to photograph reflections, for mountain weather is typically calm then and the waters still. The most perfect reflections occur on relatively small ponds and pools; on larger bodies of water there is a greater opportunity for ripples and waves to break the surface. Afternoons in the mountains are best left to activities other than photographing reflections, because storms and winds often stir water surfaces and bright mid-day light creates glare, diffusing the intensity of reflections.

Rippling waters are not a total loss, however, for water in motion can make impressionistic images. Some of the most beautiful reflections are so surreal that one cannot immediately discern the actual object or land form being reflected. The patterns of color can be as scrambled as a Kandinsky painting, yet contain enough designs to be extraordinarily pleasing to the eye. This order within chaos makes for great photographs as well as sublime memories.

When photographing reflections, remember that the reflected image is usually quite a bit darker than the land form itself. Therefore, take a light meter reading that is an average of the two. Fill half of the view finder with the reflection and the other half with the real thing, using this "average" reading to ensure a properly exposed photograph. You can then change the composition if you wish, but be sure keep the same meter reading.

Sunrise, high above Vallecito Creek, Weminuche Wilderness

No matter what the visual effect, all reflections are thought provoking. Who has not sat beside a pond and let his or her mind drift off into a world less demanding? Some of my own most lucid moments occur while gazing at watery reflections. Throughout this book, you will experience not only the glory of Colorado in photographs, but the thoughtful insights of talented writers influenced by the majesty and power of the natural world.

I sincerely hope that these words and images will allow you to unload some of the burdens of daily life, at least for a few moments. May they kindle a renewed sense of purpose in your life as well as a greater appreciation for things natural and primal. And may you have the opportunity to visit such places as depicted in the pages of this book — to lose yourself for a while in Colorado's watery reflections.

— John Fielder
Englewood, Colorado

Other books by John Fielder:

Colorado Waterfalls Littlebook
Colorado Aspen Trees Littlebook
Colorado Lakes & Creeks Littlebook
Colorado Wildflowers Littlebook
A Colorado Autumn
To Walk in Wilderness
Colorado, Rivers of the Rockies
Along the Colorado Trail
Colorado, Lost Places and Forgotten Words
The Complete Guide to Colorado Wilderness Areas
Colorado BLM Wildlands: A Guide to Hiking &
       Floating Colorado's Canyon Country

Also look for John Fielder's Colorado wall and engagement calendars.

Evening storm along the Green River, Browns Park National Wildlife Refuge

"Beauty is composed of many things and
never stands alone. It is part of the horizon,
blue in the distance, great primeval silences,
knowledge of things of the earth..."
— Sigurd Olson, Reflections from the North Country

Morning light on Rolling Mountain, along the Colorado Trail,
San Juan National Forest

"It is the marriage of the soul with Nature that makes the intellect fruitful, and gives birth to the imagination."
— Henry David Thoreau, Journal

❧ ❧

Alpine tarn, Weminuche Wilderness

"So rests the sky against the earth. The dark still tarn in the lap of the forest. As a husband embraces his wife in faithful tenderness, so the bare ground and trees are embraced by the still, high light of the morning."

— Dag Hammarskjöld, Markings

❧❦

Dawn at Archuleta Lake, along the Continental Divide near Wolf Creek Pass

"To see clearly is poetry, prophecy,
and religion — all in one."

— John Ruskin, Modern Painters

❧

Yule Lakes, Raggeds Wilderness

"...the world cannot be discovered by a
journey of miles, no matter how long, but only
by a spiritual journey, a journey of one inch...
by which we arrive at the ground at our feet,
and learn to be at home."

— Wendell Berry, The Unforeseen Wilderness

❧ ☙

The Twin Sisters and Bear Mountain, Andrews Lake, San Juan Mountains

Overleaf: Mount Harvard at sunset, Collegiate Peaks Wilderness

"To the attentive eye, each moment of the year
has its own beauty...it beholds, every hour,
a picture which was never seen before,
and which shall never be seen again."
— Ralph Waldo Emerson, Beauty

Sunset, Weminuche Wilderness

"Commonly we stride through the out-of-doors too swiftly to see more than the most obvious and prominent things. For observing nature, the best pace is a snail's pace."

— Edwin Way Teale, Circle of the Seasons

Uncompahgre Peak, Uncompahgre Wilderness

"If happiness consists in the number of pleasing emotions that occupy our mind — how true is it that the contemplation of nature...is one of the great sources of happiness."

— Thomas Belt, The Naturalist in Nicaragua

❧ ☙

Mount Elbert, as seen from North Halfmoon Creek,
Mount Massive Wilderness

"Now I see the secret of the making of the best
persons. It is to grow in the open air,
and to eat and sleep with the earth."

— Walt Whitman, Leaves of Grass

Autumn along the Alamosa River, Rio Grande National Forest

"Joys come from simple and natural things,
mists over the meadows, sunlight on leaves....
Even rain and wind and stormy clouds bring joy..."
— Sigurd Olson, Open Horizons

❧ ❦

Buttermilk clouds, North Colony Lakes, Sangre de Cristo Wilderness

"No matter how tightly the body may be chained
to the wheel of daily duties, the spirit is free…
to bear itself away from noise and vexations into
the secret places of the mountains."
— Frank Bolles, At the North of Bearcamp Water

Morning light on East Mineral Creek, La Garita Wilderness

"I began to reflect on Nature's eagerness to sow life everywhere....That immense, overwhelming, relentless, burning ardency of Nature for the stir of life!"
— Henry Beston, The Outermost House

❧⸾❧

Marsh marigolds, Peeler Basin, Gunnison National Forest

Overleaf: The Sawatch Range, North Halfmoon Lakes, Mount Massive Wilderness

"The visible marks of extraordinary wisdom and power appear so plainly in all the works of creation that a rational creature who will but seriously reflect on them cannot miss the discovery of a deity."

— John Locke, An Essay Concerning Human Understanding

❧❧

The Gates of Lodore, along the Green River,
Dinosaur National Monument

"Today, more than ever before, we are in need of serenity, quiet, contemplation, thoughtfulness. What we have left of wilderness can help us achieve these."

— Olaus J. Murie, The Living Wilderness

Dawn at Notch Lake, Mount Massive Wilderness

"A rock pile ceases to be a rock pile the moment
a single man contemplates it, bearing within him
the image of a cathedral."

— Antoine de Saint Exupery, Flight to Arras

❧

Sunrise on the Needles Mountains, Weminuche Wilderness

"Everybody needs beauty as well as bread, places to play in and pray in where Nature may heal and cheer and give strength to body and soul alike."

— John Muir, Travels in Alaska

Mount Yale reflected in Lake Rebecca, Collegiate Peaks Wilderness

"...much earnest philosophical thought is born of the life which springs from close association with nature."

— Laura Gilpin, The Rio Grande

The Wilson massif, from Last Dollar Road, near Telluride

"Solitude…is essential to any depth of meditation or of character; and solitude in the presence of natural beauty and grandeur is the cradle of thoughts and aspirations…"
— John Stuart Mill, Principles of Political Economy

❧ ❦

Early autumn snows, the Ruby Range, near Crested Butte

"And forget not that the earth delights to feel
your bare feet and the winds long to
play with your hair."
— Kahlil Gibran, The Prophet

❧ ❧

Sunrise along the Colorado Trail, Snow Mesa, San Juan Mountains

Overleaf: Evening thunderstorm, North Colony Lakes, Sangre de Cristo Wilderness

"Nature is shy and noncommittal in a crowd.
To learn her secrets, visit her alone or
with a single friend, at most."

— Montaigne, Essays III

❧

Cottonwood trees in autumn, Blue Mesa Reservoir, near Gunnison

"Come forth into the light of things.
Let Nature be your Teacher."

— William Wordsworth, Intimations of Immortality

❧❧

Early morning at Bushnell Lakes, Sangre de Cristo Wilderness

"Surely there is something in the unruffled calm of nature that overawes our little anxieties and doubts; the sight of the deep-blue sky…seems to impart a quiet to the mind."

— Jonathan Edwards,
The New Dictionary of Thoughts

❧⚜☙

At the confluence of the Green and Yampa rivers, Echo Park,
Dinosaur National Monument

"If you want inner peace find it in solitude…and
if you would find yourself,
look to the land from which you came
and which you go."
— Stewart L. Udall, The Quiet Crisis

Autumn colors, White River National Forest

Overleaf: Twin Lakes, above Chicago Basin, Weminuche Wilderness